About Marine Mammals

A Guide for Children

Cathryn Sill

Illustrated by John Sill

PEACHTREE

ATLANTA

For the One who created marine mammals.

—*Genesis* 1:21

Ω

Published by
PEACHTREE PUBLISHERS
1700 Chattahoochee Avenue
Atlanta, Georgia 30318-2112
www.peachtree-online.com

Text © 2016 Cathryn P. Sill
Jacket and interior illustrations © 2016 John C. Sill

Illustrations created in watercolor on archival quality 100 percent rag watercolor paper
Text and titles set in Novarese from Adobe

Printed in 2016 by Imago in Singapore

10 9 8 7 6 5 4 3 2 1
First edition

ISBN 978-1-56145-906-3

Library of Congress Cataloging-in-Publication Data

Names: Sill, Cathryn P., 1953- author. | Sill, John, illustrator.
Title: About marine mammals : a guide for children / Cathryn Sill ;
    illustrated by John Sill.
Description: Atlanta, GA : Peachtree Publishers, [2016] | Includes
    bibliographical references and index.
Identifiers: LCCN 2015041866 | ISBN 9781561459063 (alk. paper)
Subjects: LCSH: Marine mammals—Juvenile literature.
Classification: LCC QL713.2 .S547 2016 | DDC 599.5—dc23 LC record available at
http://lccn.loc.gov/2015041866

About Marine Mammals

Marine mammals live in oceans.

They may live in warm tropical water…

or in cold polar seas.

PLATE 3
Polar Bear

Marine mammals have long bodies.
This body shape helps them swim well.

Many can dive deep into the ocean
to hunt for food.

Most marine mammals are predators.
They hunt and eat other animals.

PLATE 6
Orca (Killer Whale)
(*also shown: Great White Shark*)

A few eat plants.

All marine mammals must come to the surface of the water to breathe air.

They have special ways to stay
warm in their cool, watery homes.

Most marine mammals have a thick layer of fat called blubber just under their skin.

Baby marine mammals drink milk
from their mother's body.

PLATE 12
Beluga

Some have a heavy fur coat.

Baby marine mammals drink milk
from their mother's body.

PLATE 12
Beluga

Many spend their whole lives in the water.

PLATE 13
Bottlenose Dolphin

Others come to shore to have their young and to rest.

Marine mammals may be small...

or huge.

Marine mammals need clean,
healthy oceans.

PLATE 17
Hawaiian Monk Seal

It is important to protect marine mammals
and the places where they live.

PLATE 18
Vaquita

Afterword

PLATE 1

There are around 125 species of marine mammals living in the world's oceans. Each species belongs to one of five groups: cetaceans (whales, dolphins, porpoises), pinnipeds (seals, sea lions, fur seals, walruses), sirenians (manatees, dugongs), sea otters, and polar bears. Marine mammals depend on the ocean for food and a way to move from place to place. Many make different sounds to communicate with each other. Humpback Whales are known for their "songs," which can be heard for miles. They live in all the oceans except for polar seas.

PLATE 2

Some marine mammals migrate to tropical waters in winter. Others, such as Spinner Dolphins, stay in warmer water all the time. Spinner Dolphins are named for their habit of leaping out of the water and spinning high in the air. They live in tropical and subtropical oceans all around the world.

PLATE 3

Many marine mammals are able to live all year in cold oceans. Floating ice in polar seas provides good resting places for some animals. Polar Bears spend a lot of time hunting for seals on ice floes. They are good swimmers and can stay for hours in the freezing water. Polar Bears live in the Arctic.

PLATE 4

Marine mammals must be able to swim well in order to find food and escape from predators. Some marine mammals use only their tail to move through the water and their fins to steer and stop. Others, such as seals and sea lions, use their paddle-shaped flippers to swim. California Sea Lions are the fastest pinnipeds. They can swim up to 25 mph (40 kph). California Sea Lions live along the western coast of North America.

PLATE 5

Some marine mammals are able to hold their breath for over an hour and search for food in deep water. The Cuvier's Beaked Whale is the deepest diving mammal. Scientists recorded one of these whales making a dive of nearly 10,000 feet (3,048 meters). Cuvier's Beaked Whales live in offshore waters in oceans worldwide.

PLATE 6

Some marine mammals hunt and eat large animals such as fish or other mammals. Others eat small crustaceans called krill. Orcas are powerful hunters that eat many things, including fish, squid, seals, seabirds, and even whales. Although they are often called "Killer Whales," they are large dolphins. Orcas live in oceans all around the world.

PLATE 7

Manatees and Dugongs are the only marine mammals that are herbivores (animals that eat plants). They have thick moveable lips with bristly whiskers that help them grasp sea grasses and other water plants. West Indian Manatees live in warm coastal waters in the southeastern United States, throughout the Caribbean, and along the northeastern coast of South America.

PLATE 8

Like all other mammals, marine mammals have lungs and cannot breathe underwater. Whales, dolphins, and porpoises breathe through blowholes located on the back of their heads. They have a muscular flap that covers their blowhole to keep water out when they dive. Dall's Porpoises sometimes swim so fast they push up a wave of water called a "rooster tail." The wave creates a hollow airspace at their blowhole that allows them to breathe as they swim fast. Dall's Porpoises live in the North Pacific Ocean.

PLATE 9

Marine mammals are warm-blooded. Their body temperature needs to stay the same whether they are in cool or warm places. Sometimes hundreds of them gather together on shore or ice floes to sunbathe. Walruses live in Arctic waters close to the ice pack.

PLATE 10

Blubber is a special kind of fat. It keeps marine mammals warm, stores nutrients for energy, and helps them float. Blubber on mammals found in the Arctic and Antarctic regions can be up to 12 inches (30.48 cm) thick. Southern Right Whales got their name from whalers because they considered them to be the "right" whales to hunt. Their blubber was used to make products such as soap and fuel for oil-burning lamps. Southern Right Whales live in oceans in the southern part of the world.

PLATE 11

Fur seals get their name from their thick fur. They have waterproof underfur that helps them stay dry and warm. Hunting for South American Fur Seals began hundreds of years ago and lasted until the 1980s. People hunted them for their fur, skin, and oil. South American Fur Seals live on the southern Atlantic and Pacific coasts of South America.

PLATE 12

Some marine mammals (seals and sea lions, for example) nurse their babies on land or ice. Cetaceans feed their young in the water. Baby Belugas, as well as other baby whales and dolphins, do not have lips to help them suck milk. They are able to roll their tongues like a straw and attach it to their mother's nipple. The mother can then squirt the milk from her body into the baby's mouth. Belugas live in the Arctic Ocean.

PLATE 13
Marine mammals born in the water are usually born tail first. This keeps their blowhole out of the water for as long as possible so they won't drown. Newborns must reach the surface of the water quickly to get air to breathe. Young Bottlenose Dolphins stay with their mothers for up to five years. Bottlenose Dolphins live in tropical and temperate oceans around the world.

PLATE 14
Some pinnipeds use their flippers for feet when they are on land. Others such as Harbor Seals "walk" by flopping along on their bellies. Baby Harbor Seals learn to crawl and swim very quickly after being born. They nurse on land and in water. Harbor Seals live in coastal areas north of the equator in both the Pacific and Atlantic Oceans. They are the most wide-spread pinniped.

PLATE 15
Marine mammals range in length from about 4 feet (1.2 m) to around 100 feet (30.5 m). Sea Otters are one of the smallest marine mammals. They are 3.9 to 4.9 feet (1.1 to 1.5 m) long. They do not have blubber. They have one of the warmest and thickest fur coats of any mammal. The hairs in their coats grow so close together the cold water cannot reach their skin. For many years hunters killed Sea Otters so they could sell their fur for clothing. Sea Otters are now listed as endangered. They live in coastal areas of the northern Pacific Ocean.

PLATE 16

The largest animal in the world is a marine mammal. Blue Whales are the heaviest and possibly the longest animals to have ever lived on Earth. Adults can be up to 100 feet (30.5 m) long and weigh more than 400,000 pounds (180,000 kg). Baby Blue Whales are 25 feet (7.6 m) long and may weigh over 6,000 pounds (2,722 kg) when they are born. Mother Blue Whales make around 50 gallons (227 liters) of milk each day and the calves gain over 200 pounds (91 kilograms) a day. Blue Whales live in all the oceans.

PLATE 17

Pollution from many sources is seriously threatening the health of the oceans. For years people thought that because oceans were so big it would not cause a problem to dump trash in them. Now we know that plastic thrown into the seas causes the death of more than 100,000 marine mammals each year. Trash in the oceans causes problems when animals like endangered Hawaiian Monk Seals get tangled in it or eat it by mistake. Hawaiian Monk Seals live in the northwestern Hawaiian Islands.

PLATE 18

Marine mammals are beneficial in many ways. They hunt certain ocean animals, keeping them from becoming too numerous. Scientific studies of marine mammals have led to important discoveries. Whale watching provides jobs and money for communities. People should take care not to harm marine mammals. Irresponsible fishing methods often accidentally destroy fish and other animals. This behavior is causing a shortage of food for marine animals as well as people. Vaquitas are small porpoises that can get caught in fishing nets and drown. There are probably fewer than a hundred of them left alive. Vaquitas live in the northern end of the Gulf of California, Mexico. Scientists are working together on a plan to protect Vaquitas, but it may already be too late to save them from extinction.

GLOSSARY

cetacean—the group of animals that includes whales, dolphins, and porpoises

endangered—threatened with becoming extinct

extinct—a species of animals or plants with no living members (no longer existing)

habitat—the place where animals and plants live and grow

mammal—a warm-blooded animal that has a backbone and nurses its young with milk; most mammals have hair or fur on their skin

marine—having to do with or living in the ocean

native—an animal or plant that lives naturally in a place

nutrient—a substance needed by animals and plants to live and grow

pinniped—the group of animals that includes seals, sea lions, and walruses

predator—an animal that lives by hunting and eating other animals

sirenian—the group of plant-eating marine mammals that includes manatees and dugongs

species—a group of animals or plants that are alike in many ways

temperate—not very hot and not very cold

tropical—the area near the equator that is hot year-round

SUGGESTIONS FOR FURTHER READING

BOOKS

EYE TO EYE WITH ANIMALS: MARVELOUS MARINE MAMMALS by Ruth Owen (Windmill Books)

WHAT IS A MARINE MAMMAL? (THE SCIENCE OF LIVING THINGS) by Bobbie Kalman and Jacqueline Langille (Crabtree Publishing Co.)

EYE WONDER: WHALES AND DOLPHINS by DK Publishing (DK Children)

WEBSITES

www.marinebio.org/oceans/marine-mammals
www.nmfs.noaa.gov/pr/species/mammals
www.nmmf.org/fun-facts-for-students.html
www.whalefacts.org/what-is-a-marine-mammal

RESOURCES ESPECIALLY HELPFUL IN DEVELOPING THIS BOOK

PRINCETON FIELD GUIDES: WHALES, DOLPHINS, AND OTHER MARINE MAMMALS OF THE WORLD by Hadoram Shirihai and Brett Jarrett (Princeton University Press)

NATIONAL AUDUBON SOCIETY: GUIDE TO MARINE MAMMALS OF THE WORLD by Randall Reeves, Brent S. Stewart, Phillip J. Clapham, and James A. Powell (Alfred A. Knopf)

ABOUT... SERIES

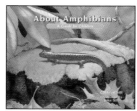

978-1-56145-234-7 HC
978-1-56145-312-2 PB

978-1-56145-038-1 HC
978-1-56145-364-1 PB

978-1-56145-688-8 HC
978-1-56145-699-4 PB

978-1-56145-301-6 HC
978-1-56145-405-1 PB

978-1-56145-256-9 HC
978-1-56145-335-1 PB

978-1-56145-588-1 HC
978-1-56145-837-0 PB

978-1-56145-881-3 HC
978-1-56145-882-0 PB

978-1-56145-757-1 HC
978-1-56145-758-8 PB

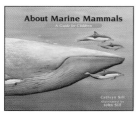

978-1-56145-906-3 HC

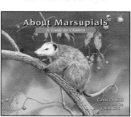

978-1-56145-358-0 HC
978-1-56145-407-5 PB

978-1-56145-331-3 HC
978-1-56145-406-8 PB

978-1-56145-795-3 HC

978-1-56145-743-4 HC
978-1-56145-741-0 PB

978-1-56145-536-2 HC
978-1-56145-811-0 PB

978-1-56145-907-0 HC
978-1-56145-908-7 PB

978-1-56145-454-9 HC
978-1-56145-914-8 PB

ALSO AVAILABLE IN BILINGUAL EDITION

• About Birds / Sobre los pájaros / 978-1-56145-783-0 PB • About Mammals / Sobre los mamíferos / 978-1-56145-800-4 PB
• About Insects / Sobre los insectos / 978-1-56145-883-7 PB • About Reptiles / Sobre los reptiles / 978-1-56145-909-4 PB

Deserts

ISBN 978-1-56145-641-3 HC
ISBN 978-1-56145-636-9 PB

Forests

ISBN 978-1-56145-734-2 HC

Grasslands

ISBN 978-1-56145-559-1 HC

Mountains

ISBN 978-1-56145-469-3 HC
ISBN 978-1-56145-731-1 PB

Oceans

ISBN 978-1-56145-618-5 HC
ISBN 978-1-56145-960-5 PB

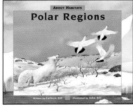

Polar Regions

ISBN 978-1-56145-832-5 HC

Wetlands

ISBN 978-1-56145-432-7 HC
ISBN 978-1-56145-689-5 PB

THE SILLS

CATHRYN AND JOHN SILL are the dynamic team who created the About… series as well as the About Habitats series. Their books have garnered praise from educators and have won a variety of awards, including Bank Street Best Books, CCBC Choices, NSTA/CBC Outstanding Science Trade Books for Students K–12, Orbis Pictus Recommended, and Science Books and Films Best Books of the Year. Cathryn, a graduate of Western Carolina State University, taught early elementary school classes for thirty years. John holds a BS in wildlife biology from North Carolina State University. Combining his artistic skill and knowledge of wildlife, he has achieved an impressive reputation as a wildlife artist. The Sills live in Franklin, North Carolina.

Fred Eldredge, Creative Image Photography